Jane Austen

VIP

Very Interesting People

*Bite-sized biographies of Britain's most
fascinating historical figures*

Jane Austen

Very Interesting People

Marilyn Butler

OXFORD
UNIVERSITY PRESS

OXFORD
UNIVERSITY PRESS

Great Clarendon Street, Oxford OX2 6DP

Oxford University Press is a department of the University of Oxford.
It furthers the University's objective of excellence in research, scholarship,
and education by publishing worldwide in

Oxford New York

Auckland Cape Town Dar es Salaam Hong Kong Karachi
Kuala Lumpur Madrid Melbourne Mexico City Nairobi
New Delhi Shanghai Taipei Toronto

With offices in

Argentina Austria Brazil Chile Czech Republic France Greece
Guatemala Hungary Italy Japan Poland Portugal Singapore
South Korea Switzerland Thailand Turkey Ukraine Vietnam

Oxford is a registered trade mark of Oxford University Press
in the UK and in certain other countries

Published in the United States
by Oxford University Press Inc., New York

First published in the *Oxford Dictionary of National Biography* 2004
This paperback edition first published 2007

© Oxford University Press 2007

Database right Oxford University Press (maker)

First published 2007

British Library Cataloguing in Publication Data

Data available

Library of Congress Cataloging in Publication Data

Data available

Typeset by SPI Publisher Services, Pondicherry, India
Printed in Great Britain
on acid-free paper by
Ashford Colour Press Ltd, Gosport, Hampshire

ISBN 978–0–19–921760–1 (Pbk.)

10 9 8 7 6 5 4 3 2 1

Contents

About the author

Marilyn Butler specializes in the study of late eighteenth- and early nineteenth-century literature and is the former Rector of Exeter College, Oxford (1993–2004). Between 1986 and 1993 she was King Edward VII Professor of English Literature at the University of Cambridge. She is the author of *Jane Austen and the War of Ideas* (1975) and has edited or introduced editions of *Mansfield Park*, *Emma*, and *Northanger Abbey*. Her other publications include *Romantics, Rebels and Reactionaries* (1981) and (as editor) *The Works of Maria Edgeworth* (1999–2003).

Childhood

1

Jane Austen (1775–1817),

novelist, was born on 16 December 1775 at the rectory in Steventon, near Basingstoke, Hampshire, the seventh child and younger daughter of George Austen (1731–1805), rector of Deane and Steventon, and private tutor, and his wife, Cassandra (1739–1827), youngest daughter of the Revd Thomas Leigh (1696–1764) and Jane Walker (*d*. 1768).

The Austens and the Leighs

George Austen was the only son of William Austen (1701–1737), a surgeon of Tonbridge, Kent, and Rebecca, daughter of the Gloucester physician

Sir George Hampson, baronet, who died in 1733. When William Austen died less than five years later, the responsibility for George and his sisters Philadelphia (1730–1792) and Leonora (1732–1783) was shouldered by their uncle Francis Austen (1698–1791). George was educated at Tonbridge School at his uncle's expense, and thereafter by a scholarship at St John's College, Oxford. He was ordained deacon at Oxford in March 1754 and priest at Rochester, Kent, in May 1755. Returning to Kent renewed George's contacts with his uncle Francis, who by the early 1750s had become an influential figure in county affairs. He easily arranged for George to serve as a curate at Shipbourne, near Tonbridge, and as an assistant master at his old school.

In 1761 another family benefactor, Thomas Knight of Godmersham, Kent, presented George to the living of Steventon, Hampshire. Francis Austen purchased two livings adjacent to Steventon, Deane and Ashe, so that George could take on the first to fall vacant (this would be Deane in 1773). Absent for the first few years, George's move to Steventon in 1764 was prompted by his marriage to Cassandra Leigh, whom he probably met at Oxford. Cassandra came from a large family of prosperous clerics and successful Oxford scholars. Her father, a fellow of All Souls College, Oxford, was rector of Harpsden, Oxfordshire, and her mother was connected to the wealthy and old-established Oxfordshire family of Perrot. From their great-aunt Anne Perrot, Cassandra and her sister Jane (1736–1783) each inherited £200, while a moderate fortune went at sixteen to their brother James (1735–1817), who now added 'Perrot' to his name. Her younger brother Thomas (1747–1821) was born with a mental disability, and was cared for outside the family circle.

George Austen and Cassandra Leigh were married on 26 April 1764 at St Swithin's Church, Bath, and moved first into the rectory at Deane, which was vacant; Steventon's was dilapidated. They had six sons: James (1765–1819), who became a curate and was rector of Steventon from his father's death; George (1766–1838), who was epileptic, and at six was sent to join Cassandra's brother Thomas;

Edward (1767–1852), who in 1783 became heir to the property of his second cousin Thomas Knight, took his name, and was the steady benefactor of his mother, brothers, and sisters; Henry Thomas (1771–1850), militia officer, banker, entrepreneur, and finally clergyman; and Francis William (Frank) (1774–1865), and Charles John (1779–1852), who both entered the navy and rose to be admirals. Their elder daughter, Cassandra Elizabeth (1773–1845), died unmarried as did Jane.

George Austen and his wife each inherited about £1000 during their early married years. With a growing family they moved in 1768 to the Steventon rectory, but found that they were living beyond their means. Immediate help came from a legacy left by Cassandra's mother, which her brother, James Leigh-Perrot, a trustee, released for the couple to invest. In 1773 George decided to take boys 'of good family' as boarders, preparing them for university, where they would meet a largely classical syllabus. Meanwhile his wife, kept a bull and cows and grew vegetables in order to feed their large household. Cheerful and optimistic like her husband, Cassandra lacked formal education but had a homespun wit, and for thirty years managed her domestic world competently and energetically.

Home life and education

Jane Austen was born a month later than her parents expected; like the other Austen children, she was baptized at Steventon rectory on the day of her birth by George Austen. The formal ceremony took place on 5 April 1776 at St Nicholas's Church, which stood on the rising ground behind the rectory. The Austens' resident children divided into two groups. The three eldest boys (not counting George) commanded respect from the younger ones and were being prepared, like their father and maternal grandfather, for Oxford University. The boys qualified, on Cassandra's side, as 'founder's kin' at St John's College, which entitled them against competition to free tuition. Edward did not go. He was adopted instead by Thomas Knight and his wife Catherine, and sent for four years on the grand tour of Europe to qualify him for the life of a landed gentleman in the Austens' native Kent. The younger group, two girls and two boys, formed a companionable and less competitive little community under the effective leadership of the practical, self-confident Cassandra, who from an early age could hold her own in adult company. Both parents and the trio of older boys seem to have been kind to the little ones, who were all healthy and active.

The standard picture of Jane Austen's happy childhood in a pastoral idyll derives from her nephew (James) Edward Austen-Leigh (1798–1874), who with the help of his half-sister Anna Austen (later Lefroy; 1793–1872) and sister Caroline Austen (1805–1880) wrote the first extended memoir of the author (1870). Edward evoked the big, rather shabby, three-storey house, the kitchen gardens, the farmyard, and a grassy bank down which children could roll. In the evenings the parents joined their children in board games, card games, puzzles, and charades. From time to time they entertained neighbours—and when the boarders were absent, house guests—to dinner. Both adults and children enjoyed dancing afterwards. When on their own they read aloud, often novels, to the circle before bedtime. (Nothing is said in the *Memoir* of Jane's performances of her juvenilia.) Mrs Austen and the two girls sewed dresses for themselves, shirts for the brothers. From 1782 to 1789 there were theatricals, almost without exception comedies then in the stage repertory, invariably produced by James.

The *Memoir* reveals that the family could be obtuse about the two sisters, though more perspicacious in the case of the brothers. Mrs Austen almost always spoke of 'the girls' as a pair or, if forced to single out Jane, mentioned her attachment to her sister. Anna Lefroy remembered her grandmother saying that 'if Cassandra were going to have her head cut off, Jane would insist on sharing her fate' (Austen-Leigh, *Memoir*, chap. 1). George and Cassandra Austen valued family cohesion, which led them to indulge the very young Jane in her reluctance to be parted from her sister. As Cassandra grew up, this was sometimes difficult for Jane herself. Chronically shy in early adolescence, she compensated by remaining silent, or by showing off, speaking affectedly, and conspicuously flirting. Observers commented on her unpredictability in public, to which Jane lightly confessed in the earliest of her letters to Cassandra that survive. The family barely referred to her awkwardness in society. On the contrary, one former member recalled that while Cassandra 'had the *merit* of having her temper always under command', Jane had 'the *happiness* of a temper that never required to be commanded' (ibid., chap. 1). Cassandra, who knew her best, received letters in which Jane sounded dissatisfied with her lot, impatient, angry, or unhappy: 'Theo... came back in time to shew his usual, nothing-meaning, harmless, heartless Civility' (*Letters*, 179); 'the Lances...live in a handsome style and are rich, and she [Mrs Lance] seemed to like to be rich...she will soon feel therefore that we are not worth her acquaintance' (ibid., 117).

Serious, judicious, and familial, Jane's nephew Edward saw his aunt and her talent for writing as part of a rounded family achievement. Their scholarly father educated his daughters as well as his sons, and the older brothers discussed books with the younger children. Edward commented that 'she certainly enjoyed that important element of mental training, associating at home with persons of cultivated intellect' (Austen-Leigh, *Memoir*, chap. 3). Even so, in spring 1783, at the very age when Jane could read for herself, her parents despatched their daughters and their cousin Jane Cooper to Oxford to be tutored, with apparently little aptitude, by Mrs Ann Cawley, the widow of a former principal of Brasenose College and a sister of the Revd Dr Edward Cooper (Mrs Austen's kinsman by marriage). Jane did not get on well with Mrs Cawley. In the girls' second term (summer to autumn 1783), without informing their parents, she moved her pupils to Southampton, presumably to economize. The sea port was in the grip of an epidemic, probably typhoid, which all three girls caught. After Jane Cooper managed to get a message home, the two mothers came to fetch their daughters away. The girls recovered, but Mrs Cooper caught the disease and died on 25 October 1783.

Despite this miserable experience, after they had spent a further year at home George Austen decided that his daughters should attend the Abbey House School, Reading, from spring 1785 to December 1786. It was a boarding-school patronized by wealthy merchants and tradesmen, and in the mornings offered instruction in English (including spelling but not punctuation), French, some Italian, history, and needlework. There were dancing classes, and some special end-of-half-year events such as theatricals and recitations, which the headmistress organized jointly with the adjoining boys' school, Valpy's. But other Abbey House girls afterwards best remembered the school for its long leisurely afternoons, allowing visits to the nearby lending library, which catered adeptly for the tastes and imaginations of girls and young women by way of romance, adventure, and much male greed and villainy.

The making of a writer

Society and theatricals

In his *Memoir of Jane Austen*, Edward Austen-Leigh planted the tradition, subscribed to by most twentieth-century critics and biographers, that Austen the novelist was substantially created at home. Thanks to tuition by her father and brothers, Jane was exposed as a child to the eighteenth-century essayists Joseph Addison, Richard Steele, and Samuel Johnson and to the novelists Samuel Richardson and Fanny Burney. It is probably true that the clarity, sharpness, and wit of the prose of Austen's juvenilia indicate attentive reading in the century's stylists, a good ear for the balance of a sentence, and sound regard for verbal economy. Her seniors did right by her on these counts, but they cannot have done everything. Austen's immersion in contemporary popular fiction began at school and was equally fundamental. At the Abbey House School she amused herself as her socially mixed classmates did in following the adventures and trials of modern woman, as these were purveyed most readily and cheaply in a handful of specialist magazines, such as George Robinson's monthly miscellany, the *Lady's Magazine* (established 1770). In his first issue Robinson boasted that he catered for the widest possible range of taste, status, and income, from a duchess to a newly literate housemaid. In each issue from a quarter to a third of the space was likely to be occupied by fiction, much of it sent in by readers, who might set their narratives in stylized exotic worlds or in common domestic life among the middling sort. But the standard plotline for most longer fiction, whether published in multi-volume book form or serialized in a magazine, was the courtship of lovers of unequal rank and means, involving the woman particularly in picaresque adventures and trials, with a happy ending always in jeopardy from the economic and social differences between the protagonists. Austen's first three novels conform to these archetypal features of the fiction of the 1780s and 1790s.

At the age of eleven, however, Jane Austen was not concerned with novels but with reinstating herself among the people and activities of the crowded rectory at Steventon. In December 1786 Jane and Cassandra left school for good, to find a household populated with exotic visitors. Their father's sister Philadelphia Hancock had brought to Steventon her 25-year-old daughter Eliza (1761–1813) who, by her marriage in 1781, had become Comtesse Eliza de Feuillide. Eliza's experiences in Paris and Versailles, where she had attended court, had given her style, polish, and the French language, almost irresistible attractions for her young Steventon cousins; she had also performed amateur dramatics at the family home near Nérac in south-west France. With a trust set up for her as a child by Warren Hastings, governor-general of Bengal and a friend of her parents, Eliza was able to lead an independent life in Paris, London, and

the English resort towns of Bath and Tunbridge
Wells. But, family-minded like other Austens,
Eliza also became over the next decade a frequent
visitor to Steventon and a powerful influence on
her cousins, the girls as well as the boys.

Jane Austen, her sister, and even her brother
Henry 'came out' socially while under the wing
of their exotic cousin Eliza. Her hospitality in
the West End houses she rented, her tireless
mobility, and her appetite for flirtation were never
more in evidence than in the year in which
she made plans for an ambitious theatrical pro-
gramme at Steventon the following Christmas,
1787. Eliza was already well briefed in the play-
wright Hannah Cowley's recent London stage
successes, beginning with *The Belle's Stratagem*
(1780), which had two vigorous and intelligent
female roles, and an undoubtedly feminist message. It was, however, Lady Bell Bloomer, the
intelligent and kindly heroine of Cowley's *Which
is the Man?* (1783), that Eliza had studied, by spon-
soring a performance of the play at Tunbridge
Wells Theatre in September 1787, and that she

meant to act at Steventon. Unfortunately Eliza's plans included a part for a Kent cousin of about her own age, Philadelphia (Phila) Walter, who positively refused to act. She was taken at Steventon to have an objection to the particular play, or to acting on principle. Eliza with her customary amiability gave up her choice of play, and a safe old favourite, Susanna Centlivre's *The Wonder: a Woman Keeps a Secret* (1714), was chosen instead, with James producing, Henry the leading man, and Eliza the leading woman. By comparison with the jealous resentments of the Bertram family in *Mansfield Park*, the Steventon theatricals of 1787 appear to have passed off decorously, except that Cassandra and Jane were on hand to observe Eliza flirting finely with both James and Henry during the rehearsals and performances of a mildly saucy play.

The following year was busy theatrically, but it was also the last season, because all the brothers but Charles had left home. After Eliza returned to London, Henry Fielding's burlesque *The Tragedy of Tragedies, or, The Life and Death of Tom Thumb the Great* (1731) was performed in March 1788. James Townley's rumbustious *High Life Below Stairs* (1759) and Isaac Bickerstaff's farce *The Sultan* (1775), a likely future source for *Pride and Prejudice*, followed at the end of the year. The first of the three projects parodies the exaggerated conventions and rhetoric of John Dryden's heroic dramas, and, in a new contemporary version, ends with a battle scene in which the entire cast dies, orating as they fall. The other two have popular settings and situations: servants take on the roles of their masters; or an Englishwoman, finding herself a captive in a harem, cheekily teaches the sultan how to become agreeable to his subjects. Traces of the knockabout humour, caricature, and mockery calculated to please adolescent schoolboy boarders are evident in the plays put on in 1788 largely for their amusement, but Cassandra and Jane also took part.

Austen's juvenilia

From early 1787 to June 1793 Jane wrote a large number of sketches, burlesque playlets (which may have been acted by others or by herself), epistolary novellas, and short picaresque adventures. Usually they were dedicated to a member of the household. Those she wished to keep she copied into three blank copy-books given to her by her father, which she named 'Volume the First', 'Volume the Second', and 'Volume the Third'. The twenty-seven pieces in these copy-books resemble exercises in many kinds of literary form, and they had a function, since they were read out to or more likely performed for the family audience by the author, who was, according to her brother Henry, a confident speaker and a natural comic. Unfortunately there is no direct description of her performances, and since none is dedicated to boarders it seems likely that they were excluded. All the same, boarders were taken in at Steventon until 1796, and the presence in the house of adolescent boys, as well as her youngest brother, Charles, is worth considering as an almost certain influence on her early writing.

The juvenilia are full of self-confident and errant young women: Laura, Elfrida, Alice, the

'Beautifull Cassandra' (a milliner's daughter), and Charlotte Lutterell at Lesley Castle. There is something of Austen herself in all the heroines of her mature novels, and, surely, also in the bold, energized adventuresses of the juvenilia. It may be her physical appearance that is conveyed, or her coolness and cynicism. Rebelliousness and an anti-social impatience are qualities she confesses to in her correspondence with Cassandra, and seems to identify with in Marianne Dashwood in *Sense and Sensibility*. This intolerance of mediocrity is also the offence committed by Emma Woodhouse, 'the heroine whom no one but myself will much like' (Austen-Leigh, *Memoir*, chap. 10). These brief hints are recognizable by readers as self-portraiture and are enjoyed for this reason. An obvious case from the juvenilia is Alice Johnson of 'Jack and Alice', a heroine maddeningly badgered by Lady Williams because she has unfashionably full red cheeks, like Austen's own. A red face is also a sign of inebriety, and sure enough not just Alice but the entire Johnson family is soon alleged to be addicted to the bottle. Jane in real life probably endured jokes along these lines, and may even have found herself typecast in the production of Fielding's *Tom Thumb*, by being allotted the part of King Arthur's consort, Queen Dollalolla, a woman 'entirely faultless, saving that she is a little given to drink' and in love with Tom Thumb.

Jane Austen was always an exact writer. She alludes to specifics, from real-life people and events or from books in use in the household. Her early twentieth-century editor R. W. Chapman observed that she was 'exceptionally and even surprisingly dependent' on reality and 'family and biographical truth' as the 'basis of imaginary construction' (*Times Literary Supplement*, 10 December 1931). She was locked into family experience, as an observer of the relationships between siblings and a critic of richer members of the larger Austen and Leigh family. Her inner family circle, the three or four always on hand as an audience, could recognize, enjoy, or even correct these shared memories. No doubt her parents and her elder brothers—brought up to value quick wit and puns, and to ridicule blunders— helped to lend Austen's writing its sharpness. The brothers and their contemporaries, the boarders, may also have encouraged the interest in caricature that both Cassandra and Jane displayed in adolescence. Cassandra exercised an uncertain taste in graphic satire in her illustrations for Jane's 'History of England' (November 1791), and was perhaps joking in Jane's manner when in 1804 she sketched Jane from behind, her face hidden by a large bonnet.

Later Jane took pleasure in the role of aunt, and resumed her adolescent practice of inventing stories, games, and puzzles, now to entertain nephews and nieces. One explanation for the surreal, violent, insubordinate world of her juvenilia could be that it originated with oral tales she made up perhaps while still at school to tell other children. Here and there her adventurous plots echo oriental fantasy, Jonathan Swift's *Gulliver's Travels* (1726) and Horace Walpole's *Hieroglyphic Tales* (1785). Other current items are satirical, in the vein of burlesque and ridicule that Jane picked up from Henry Fielding and more contemporary wits, among them Fanny

Burney. Members of the household, including the boarders, would be as familiar as she was with the books in her father's circumscribed library. Oliver Goldsmith's *History of England* (1771) and especially Samuel Richardson's *Sir Charles Grandison* (1753–4) offered a fine opportunity for parody, a form that required a knowing audience, or simply challenged young readers to identify a source. Throughout her writing career Austen teased and puzzled her readers by mimicking other novelists, recycling and neatly improving on her materials, amusing readers who could still spot the original—devices learned at home to activate her readers of school age and make them her allies.

Austen's three volumes of juvenilia constitute a miscellany of the conventions and clichés of late eighteenth-century fiction, drama, and stage farce: they contain characters, incidents, and scenes out of a largely picaresque tradition, straight or comic; stereotypical fools or villains from different ends of the social scale; haughty or cruel aristocrats and parents, conceited young males, pleasure-seeking women. Only in

'Catharine, or the Bower' (dedication dated August 1792, 'Volume the Third') does Austen at this stage employ the central convention of the novel, a sympathetic protagonist. More typically it is the scenic aspect and broad brush of eighteenth-century novels, their vivid social panorama, that is evoked by Austen's crowd of minor characters, and their familiar venues: the visit, the day excursion, the journey, the spa, the ball, along with a short list of dramatic incidents, such as an accident to a carriage or a boat, a robbery, or a murder. Jane Austen's tastes were at this time as tomboyish as the vigorous practices she attributes in *Northanger Abbey* to Catherine Morland—of rolling down the grassy bank behind the house, and playing cricket with the boys.

Courtship and company

In summer 1788 the Steventon Austens decided that it would be a timely gesture to visit George's uncle and boyhood patron 'Old Francis' Austen. Cassandra at fifteen and a half could be described as of an age to 'come out'. And if she went, then

Jane, though only twelve and a half, must also go. On 21 July Francis gave a grand dinner at the Red House, his handsome Georgian home in Sevenoaks, Kent, for them to meet their second cousins and contemporaries from the senior and wealthiest branch of Kent Austens, later known as the Austens of Kippington. The occasion must have been gruelling for Jane, if, as seems likely, it is recalled by the dinner party at the Grants' rectory in *Mansfield Park*. Here Fanny Price, who suffers from agonizing shyness, is put through a series of 'coming-out' occasions, though, like her creator at twelve, she dreads conversing with strangers. As more and more strangers appear Fanny tells herself that numbers help, 'since every addition to the party must rather forward her favourite indulgence of being suffered to sit silent and unattended to' (vol. 2, chap. 5). Yet Jane at the Red House was not silent enough, according to her cousin the censorious Phila Walter. But Phila already knew something to the discredit of Jane's brother Henry (the vigorous flirtation he had conducted with Eliza for a year and a half), and seemed determined to dislike the Austen sisters. She compared Cassandra to herself:

> As it's pure Nature to love ourselves I may be allowed to give the preference to the Eldest who is generally reckoned a most striking resemblance of me in features, complexion & manners. I never found myself so disposed to be vain, as I can't help thinking her very pretty.

Jane, however, was barely tolerable. Phila's assessment is the first full description of her behaviour in company: 'The youngest (Jane) is very like her brother Henry, not at all pretty & very prim, unlike a girl of twelve' (*Austen Papers*, 131). Phila completed her résumé of the family by noting: 'My aunt has lost several fore-teeth which makes her look old; my uncle is quite white-haired, but looks vastly well: all in high spirits & disposed to be pleased with each other'. On the following day Phila entertained the Steventon Austens at her home, Seal, and revoked her criticism of the younger Cassandra. 'She keeps up conversation in a very sensible & pleasing manner.' Otherwise

her first impressions stuck: 'Jane is whimsical &
affected' (ibid.).

From 1791 to the summer of 1793, when Jane
Austen wrote the last of her juvenilia, the
Steventon Austens experienced a season of marriages in the family, which was also darkened
by several deaths. In December 1791 Jane's
brother Edward married Elizabeth Bridges, from
a wealthy Kent family, and in March 1792 James
married Anne Mathew, daughter of a general
and granddaughter of a duke. About this time
the most significant union of all for the Austen
sisters occurred, Cassandra's engagement to one
of George Austen's pupils, Tom Fowle, who, as
verses by Mrs Austen show, was and continued
to be a family favourite. Old Francis Austen died
on 21 June 1791. Sympathetic and watchful of
deserving young relatives in the past, Francis had
in his last arrangements followed the established
practice of concentrating the family capital on his
eldest son and male heirs. As a partial exception
George Austen received £500. In an exchange of
letters later that summer between Mrs Cassandra

Austen and her sister-in-law Philadelphia Hancock, with Eliza participating, the bitterness of
Francis's overlooked nieces and great-nieces was
vigorously expressed. They saw his policy as poor
recompense for the attention and care the old man
had received from his female relatives, and his
largess redundant in relation to Francis Motley
Austen, who was, Eliza wrote, 'immensely rich
before' (1 August 1791, *Austen Papers*, 143).

With scant further prospects of a legacy from
Kent, Jane's parents seriously turned their attention in the 1790s to the nearest of the Oxfordshire Leigh connections, Mrs Austen's childless
brother, James Leigh-Perrot, and his wife, Jane
née Cholmeley, heiress of a Lincolnshire family
of Atlantic traders long resident and prominent
in Barbados. In 1793 their parents pressed Jane
and Cassandra in vain to visit the couple in
Bath. In the privacy of letters to Cassandra in
the 1790s and 1800s, Jane often showed reluctance to visit unfamiliar cousins, such as her
mother's connections the literary Cookes of Great
Bookham. Fanny Burney, then Austen's favourite

contemporary author, was living there in a pic-
turesque area close to Boxhill. It had become a
refuge for French aristocrats fleeing the revolution. Germaine de Staël, her lover Narbonne, and
General D'Arblay, who married Burney in July
1793, visited Bookham at this time. Jane still felt
shy at parties full of strangers and, now that she
paid visits every second year at least to her brother
Edward in Kent, she was made keenly aware of
the social gap between 'East Kent wealth' and
economies at the Steventon rectory. 'Kent is the
only place for happiness. Everybody is rich there',
she wrote sourly to Cassandra (*Letters*, 28), and,
when her parents moved to a yet more unfashion-
able early dinner hour, 'half after Three...I am
afraid you will despise us' (ibid., 27).

By 1795 Cassandra's long-standing engagement to
Tom Fowle had become increasingly frustrating.
Although his kinsman Lord Craven, commander-
in-chief of the British expeditionary force to the
West Indies, had offered him a living at Allington,
near Amesbury, Wiltshire, the income could not
support a wife and family. In January 1796 Tom

accompanied Craven to the West Indies where he had a wealthy uncle who died that summer. Tom himself died of yellow fever on his return journey in February 1797 and was buried at sea off St Domingo. He left Cassandra his savings of £1000.

Up to that time, especially in the correspondence of Eliza de Feuillide, the Austen sisters—particularly the poised, good-looking Cassandra—were thought marriageable with or without a dowry. In her letters to Cassandra, Jane joked about flirtations, and about young men with dark eyes who were, she claimed, in love with Cassandra, or more rarely with herself. One such suitor was Tom Lefroy (1776–1869), the Irish nephew of (Isaac Peter) George Lefroy, rector of Ashe. The rector's wife, Anne, usually known as Madam Lefroy, was a cultivated woman with some scientific as well as literary interests. She was both a stimulating teacher who widened Jane's taste in poetry, and a sympathetic listener to whom Jane went for advice. Between 1795 and 1796 Jane flirted with Tom Lefroy, and enjoyed reporting her progress to Cassandra in the earl-iest of her lively intimate letters to her sister that survive: 'Imagine to yourself everything most profligate and shocking in the way of dancing and sitting down together', she wrote on 9–10 January 1796 (*Letters*, 1). But if Jane hoped for her friend's blessing on the rapidly developing romance, she was quickly disabused: Madam Lefroy was suffi-ciently alarmed to send Tom precipitately back to London. Jane was also flirting with Tom Fowle's younger brother Charles, another former boarder, shortly before Tom left for the West Indies. Most of this was unserious. The loss of Tom Fowle was not. Cassandra did not contemplate another attachment, and her decision came in due course to stand for Jane as well.

Early novels

Austen's laughing comedy

Having copied and put away her miscellany of
juvenilia in June 1793, Jane Austen began work
on 'Elinor and Marianne', a very early version
of *Sense and Sensibility*, said to have been first
written in an epistolary form, and read out to the
family about 1795. It was possibly at this time
that Austen also began her novella, *Lady Susan*,
although the fair copy of manuscript (now in the
Pierpont Morgan Library, New York) is untitled
and was written on paper of which two leaves
are watermarked '1805'. A spirited depiction of
a woman seeking self-advancement, *Lady Susan*
was first published as an addition to the second
edition (1871) of Edward Austen-Leigh's *Memoir*.

In August 1796 Jane visited her brother Edward and his wife, Elizabeth, at their first home, a large farmhouse at Rowling in Kent. It was while there, or immediately after returning home that October, that she began *Pride and Prejudice* under the title 'First Impressions', perhaps as an instinctive reaction against Kent hauteur. The author was the same age as her heroine Elizabeth Bennet at the start of composition ('not one and twenty'). This, the first of her novels to be completed, was finished in August 1797, and offered by her father to the publisher Thomas Cadell on 1 November 1797 as a novel in three volumes 'about the length of Miss Burney's *Evelina*' (Austen-Leigh, *Memoir*, chap. 8). The publisher declined without asking to see the manuscript. 'First Impressions' remained a family favourite, a fact confirmed by regular rereadings by Cassandra and Jane's close friend Martha Lloyd (*Letters*, 35, 44). The title had to be changed, however, after the publication of Margaret Holford's novel *First Impressions; or the Portrait* in 1801. Austen replaced it with *Pride and Prejudice*, taking a phrase from Fanny Burney's *Cecilia* (1782) as her new title.

George Austen might have sought another publisher for Jane's 'First Impressions', but did not; Jane turned stoically to her other novel-in-waiting, the tale of the two sisters Elinor and Marianne. The treatment of scenes between two sympathetic marriageable sisters in each of these early novels must in some way have been affected by the news of Tom Fowle's death that reached Steventon about 1 May 1797, while Jane still had the closing chapters of *Pride and Prejudice* to write. But Jane seemed already to have a policy of observing the conventions of two types of stage comedy—witty or 'laughing' comedy, and the comedy of sentiment, which is likely to include pathos and touches of tragedy. Each mode had its appropriate heroine, a tender melancholic romantic for the comedy of sentiment, and conversely an independent-minded woman of the world for laughing comedy. Another convention in the theatre governs minor characters, and this too Austen observes in her early pair of novels; the comic minor characters in *Pride and Prejudice*, Mrs Bennet, Mr Collins, Lady Catherine, are broader and much more developed than their equivalents in *Sense and Sensibility*, Sir John Middleton, Mrs Jennings, Mrs Palmer, and Miss Steele.

For her laughing comedy 'First Impressions' Austen looked for an outstanding heroine in the stage tradition of comedy and farce of the 1780s, and understandably borrowed from Eliza de Feuillide's favourite, the warm, mature, and generous Lady Bell Bloomer in Cowley's *Which is the Man?* Lizzie Bennet, unheroically placed as the second of five sisters, has the intelligence of Cowley's Letitia and Lady Bell. She even takes on a similar leading role in her own domestic world, which is anarchic thanks to the idleness of her father and the limited capacities of her mother. Lizzie Bennet stands up to the uncivil Darcy and his flatterer, Miss Bingley, and loyally champions her elder sister Jane's depth of feeling for Bingley. Female camaraderie of this type was also a central theme of Susanna Centlivre's play *The Wonder*. But the relationship Austen develops between Lizzie and Darcy has a nearer model in Roxalana, heroine of Bickerstaff's farce *The Sultan*, one of the last plays acted at Steventon late in 1788. Roxalana is a sensible, self-reliant Englishwoman, unfazed by finding herself in the harem of a sultan who comes to prefer her stout advice to that of the cronies and flatterers at his court. She is by no means aristocratic, as Cowley's heroines are, but of the trading class. Osmyn the vizier reflects on this after her triumph: 'who would have thought, that a little cock'd-up nose would have overturn'd the customs of a mighty empire!' (Act 2). In fact, though *Pride and Prejudice* was recognized as a fine comedy in the mainstream tradition and was a runaway success on publication in 1813, a minority of readers throughout the nineteenth century could not stomach Lizzie's vulgar mother and aunt, still less her own pert answers to Darcy and to his aunt Lady Catherine.

Unusually for Austen, the novel is also grounded in real-life public events: southern England at the outset of a major war, when threatened with a French invasion. The circumstances are the arrival in county towns of regiments of militia from other regions, following France's declaration of war in February 1793. By the winter of

1794–5 three such regiments—the South Devonshires, Oxfordshires, and Derbyshires—were billeted in counties near north Hampshire, and they caused trouble locally through riotousness, drunkenness, lechery, and bad debts. Their senior officers were either professional soldiers or gentlemen but the men and junior officers were inexperienced and, like Lieutenant Wickham in *Pride and Prejudice*, might be disreputable. Jane's brother Henry, though intended for the church, had enlisted in the Oxfordshire militia, which was mostly billeted further south in Hampshire. Gregarious and socially ambitious, Henry fed Jane with tales about the different militias: the South Devonshires, available for her to meet in Basingstoke nearby; the superior rank and wealth of the Derbyshires' officers which ensured good billets in the county town of Hertford (the novel's Meryton); and the debacle the Oxfordshires experienced when, in the freezing winter of 1794–5, they moved to new unready barracks near Brighton and rioted to such effect that the regulars and subsequently the courts had to deal with them.

Jane Austen's enhanced social understanding of her southern English world went deeper than the mere act of tracing the movements of soldiers on the map. Disguised by their uniform, handsome young men turned out to be villains and could wreck a family's peace. *Pride and Prejudice* is a story full of movement and instability, thanks partly to the dastardly escapades of Wickham with Georgiana Darcy at Ramsgate and with Lydia Bennet at Brighton and London, and eventually as a junior officer in the regulars at Newcastle. But it also pencils in respectable social gradations, as in the case of the worthy Gardiners, the kind of City of London couple who in real life were business associates at this time of the Austen cousins, moving into mansions near Sevenoaks. To match Mr Darcy's concessions to the City, Lizzie travels to Derbyshire, is admitted to Pemberley as a mere tourist, and learns from the housekeeper that Darcy is not seen at home as an arrogant snob or despot, but as a good-natured boy who has grown up to be a protective, affectionate brother. The successful weave of the many strands of this ambitious plot is one of the causes of its lasting charm.

Sisterhood, *Sense and Sensibility*, and 'Susan'

There are signs of Jane Austen's sisterly concern and shared grieving with Cassandra in the later dialogues between Jane and Lizzie Bennet in 'First Impressions' and, more extensively, in *Sense and Sensibility* in Elinor's tender concern for her sister Marianne when she loses Willoughby and falls seriously ill. Jane Bennet is only a secondary heroine in *Pride and Prejudice*, but she fits all the stereotyped features of the classic sentimental heroine: beautiful, virtuous, domestic, and reticent. Like so many heroines, she appears to have lost her lover, Bingley, after she is traduced by his sisters, false friends to Jane, and by Darcy. When Jane thinks Bingley has gone, she stoically performs her domestic duties, as Cassandra did in Kent through her early adulthood. Family relationships and above all sisterhood are regular features of Austen's novels, but the emotion generated by a sympathetic sister's share in another's pain at the loss of a lover is more sustained and raw in these two novels of the 1790s than anywhere else in her work.

Female friendship and sisterliness are also commonly found in other women's novels of the 1790s. To fill out her plot in *Sense and Sensibility* Austen borrowed freely from Jane West's *A Gossip's Story* (1796), a novel of small-town, semi-rural living centred on two motherless sisters, Louisa and Marianne Dudley. West's Marianne contributes substantially to Austen's character of the same name: she is the younger sister, brought up by an over-indulgent grandmother, whose education has been almost entirely in romantic and poetic reading. The thoughtful and considerate Louisa has an 'informed, well-regulated mind', while Marianne's sensibilities are 'tremblingly alive to the softer passions'. Marianne is intolerant of vulgar, uneducated company, a trait that costs her friends in a village and fosters malicious gossip. A steady mature man, Henry Pelham, proposes to Marianne, but she tells her father 'he is not the tender, respectful sympathizing lover ... necessary for my future repose'. More to her liking, a gentleman called Clermont saves her from a runaway horse, and at once the romantic pair discover shared tastes—'whatever was passionate, elegant and sentimental in art, or beautiful, pensive and enchanting in nature'. Each of these episodes or features is present in the story of Marianne as Austen tells it.

Jane West's writing also conveys positive religious guidance: she advises her readers 'to expect with diffidence, enjoy with gratitude and resign with submission'. Austen steadily resists the use of religious vocabulary in fiction; but she does towards the end of the first volume of *Sense and Sensibility* introduce a rationalist, sententious strain into Elinor's conversations with Marianne and Edward Ferrars that is enough to weigh down this part of the novel. Much more successful are the late scenes in which the sisters come to see their sufferings as shared. Elinor emerges as a figure like the real-life Cassandra, selfless, reticent, enduring, the most orthodox and virtuous of the Austen heroines. Thanks to her, *Sense and Sensibility* gives a guarded but very inward account of women's tribulations, and takes its place as one of the most representative of women's classic novels in the 1790s—reasons, no doubt, why Austen preferred it in 1811 to *Pride and Prejudice* as

the novel to launch her career as a published
writer.

After one novel of laughing comedy and one
of sentimental comedy, Austen returned to burlesque. The two-volume novel she first called
'Susan'—and which was published posthumously
as *Northanger Abbey*—was, according to Cassandra, written in 1798–9. Though apparently
accepted for publication by Benjamin Crosby &
Son (it was announced as being 'in the press'
in *Flowers of Literature for 1801 & 1802*; 1803),
'Susan; a Novel' did not appear. Still in manuscript
its title was later changed to 'Catherine' following
the publication of an anonymous novel, *Susan*, in
early 1809.

The work that became *Northanger Abbey* is
a story of three potential heroines: Catherine
Morland the naïve, adventurous, daughter of a
Wiltshire parson; Isabella Thorpe, a duplicitous,
thrusting anti-heroine, first encountered in a
fashionable Bath ballroom; and Eleanor Tilney,

a stereotypical oppressed Gothic heroine, who lives with a despotic father in a converted abbey in Gloucestershire. Each sister has a brother; courtships, all but one unsuccessful, develop among the three families. Catherine does not in the end confuse the real world with one of fantasy and romance. Nor does she pretentiously imagine herself a heroine. Instead her new world is a routine series of Burneyesque disappointments— crowded ballrooms, a boring chaperone (Mrs Allen), a rude and stupid suitor (John Thorpe), and soon the suitor's clumsy attempt at a Richard-sonian abduction, with the doubtful help of his overrated carriage and very slow horse. Catherine has the sense to know from the outset that she has met a man she greatly prefers, Henry Tilney. Henry entertains her by talking to her about books, and simultaneously he entertains bookish readers by his, that is Austen's, talent for parody, notably the excellent pastiche of Ann Radcliffe's *The Romance of the Forest* (1791), merged with her *Mysteries of Udolpho* (1794), with which he regales Catherine on the journey to Northanger Abbey. The charm of the story, finally, is in the naturalness and good-heartedness of Catherine Morland; her loyalty to her brother when he is jilted by Isabella; her lack of any mercenary instincts, still less guile; her emerging solid good sense; and, not least, her sensitively drawn sisterly affection for Eleanor Tilney as well as for her brother.

In April 1809 Austen wrote to Benjamin Crosby & Son to complain of their delay in publishing 'Catherine' and to threaten to take the novel elsewhere if they did not honour their commitment. Richard Crosby replied on his father's behalf that they were not obliged to publish, but would certainly go to law if she attempted to publish elsewhere. He did, however, also offer to part with the manuscript and the copyright at the price the firm had paid, £10. Austen put the matter and the book aside and returned to it only in 1815–16. It finally came out with *Persuasion* in 1817 (published by John Murray), in Austen's corrected version but with Henry's and Cassandra's title: *Northanger Abbey*.

In 1801 George Austen suddenly determined without consultation to move his family to Bath, while his eldest son, James, took over as his curate in the parish of Steventon. Jane suspected James's second wife, Mary Lloyd (1771–1843), the sister of her friend Martha Lloyd, of persuading their parents to vacate the parsonage and of coveting some of its contents. It seems that her parents had a plan, not shared with the sisters—or not at least with Jane—to travel light and to sublet their Bath accommodation for the summer months. Arriving in May 1801, they acquired their first Bath home, 4 Sydney Place, for the three-and-three-quarter-year remnant of the lease and, while the landlord redecorated, Jane, Cassandra, and their parents set off to visit seaside towns in Devon. They may have stayed at Sidmouth and certainly went to Colyton in south Devon, paying a visit to the Revd Richard Buller, one of George Austen's former boarders. By visiting friends and relatives a great deal in these summer wanderings and possibly earning rent in Bath, the family no doubt lived economically. In 1802 Charles, on leave during the nineteen-month peace of Amiens (1802–3), accompanied them on holiday. They visited Dawlish and Teignmouth in Devon, then explored the Welsh coast, going to Tenby and perhaps as far north as Barmouth. Jane and Cassandra, still travelling with Charles, spent September and October at Godmersham with Edward and November at Steventon with James and Mary. On 25 November 1802 the sisters went at the invitation of their friends Catherine and Alethea Bigg to stay at Manydown Park, at Wootton St Lawrence, north of Basingstoke and about 6 miles from Steventon. A week after their arrival, on the evening of Thursday 2 December, Jane Austen accepted a proposal of marriage from Harris Bigg-Wither, the Bigg sisters' younger brother.

If she had gone through with a marriage to this stuttering, awkward man, six years younger than herself, Jane Austen at twenty-seven could have housed and provided for her parents, who were facing a fairly straitened old age in lodgings at Bath, and Cassandra too if she wished it. On the death of his father, Harris Bigg-Wither would have inherited Manydown, and Jane would have become its mistress. She was already comfortable in the house and with its attractive owners. But there were problems at Manydown. Harris did not get on with his father, and really wanted to remove himself with Jane or another wife to a home of his own. For whatever reason, Jane thought better of her acceptance overnight, and early the following morning she and Cassandra departed precipitately for Steventon to save further embarrassment. After a brief explanation to James and Mary, they returned with James to Bath on 4 December. Jane and Cassandra said enough to James and Mary that day for the episode to pass down to young Austen women of subsequent generations, including their niece Catherine Hubback, a daughter of the sailor brother Frank, and Caroline Austen, the sister of Edward Austen-Leigh. Mary seems to have been surprised that Jane refused so desirable an offer. Catherine Hubback gathered from letters she saw that it was 'in a momentary fit of self-delusion' that Jane accepted him—'I am sure she had no attachment to him' (Le Faye, *Family Record*, 138). Caroline as so often was more forthright. Harris was 'very plain in person—awkward, & even uncouth in manner— nothing but his size to recommend him ... one need not look about for secret reason to account for a young lady's *not* loving him' (ibid. 137). Thereafter, as David Nokes adds, 'the story became the stuff of family legend' (Nokes, 258).

It was, however, the nearest Jane Austen appears to have come to marriage. In her youth she enjoyed flirting as much as she enjoyed dancing. But it was the era in her life when she was seeing much of Eliza, another witty woman who loved to tease but also meant to retain her independence even after her marriage in December 1797 to Jane's brother Henry, Eliza's first husband having been executed in France in 1794. After Jane's death, Cassandra told the nieces the story of a man Jane met on holiday in a south-west resort in the early 1800s, who appeared seriously attached to Jane, as she was to him; they never saw him again, and only later discovered that he had died. Much the same story was retold in Sir Francis Hasting Doyle's *Reminiscences and Opinions* (1886) as emanating from a resident of Chawton, though on this occasion the lovelorn suitor was encountered by the Austens on a mythical trip to Switzerland during the peace of Amiens. In either version the tale has the flavour of Cassandra's making rather than Jane's.

Countering the sentimental stories are the many occasions in Jane's letters in which she expresses aversion from marriage and childbearing ('Poor Woman! how can she be honestly breeding again?'; *Letters*, 140), makes fun of unappealing newly-weds, or complains of spoilt and tiresome children. Of her nephew George she said: 'I shall think with tenderness & delight on his beautiful & smiling Countenance & interesting Manners, till a few years have turned him into an ungovernable, ungracious fellow' (ibid., 17). She was also a 'good aunt' to three nieces and a nephew, but these were hand-picked children old enough and thoughtful enough to share her own literary interests— James's children Anna, Edward, and Caroline, and the motherless eldest niece Fanny Knight, to whom Austen gave unsentimental advice on love and marriage. Except in the case of the Crofts in *Persuasion*, Austen in her fiction is hesitant about the long-term satisfactions of marriage. Older couples, the Sir Thomas Bertrams, the Allens, and the Bennets, have long since forgotten youthful rapture, if they ever experienced it.

Austen must have handed over the manuscript of 'Susan'—the future *Northanger Abbey*—shortly after the painful Bigg-Wither episode in December 1802. Though Catherine Morland will make an ingenuous, sweet-natured bride, Henry Tilney's reasons for pursuing her are oddly casual: 'a persuasion of her partiality for him had been the only cause of giving her a serious thought' (vol. 2, chap. 15). That is not very far from Jane's cool diagnosis, at the beginning of *Northanger Abbey*, of Mr Allen's marriage: 'Mrs Allen was one of that numerous class of females, whose society can raise no other emotion than surprise at there being any men in the world who could like them well enough to marry them' (vol. 1, chap. 2). One of the issues arising from the Bigg-Wither proposal was its bearing not only on Jane's future but on Cassandra's too. At some point the sisters must have seriously debated the possibility of a marriage of convenience rather than love, that is, a 'comfortable' establishment for one of them, which might (like Harris's proposal) provide a secure future for the other. The once-romantic Marianne's marriage to the wealthy Colonel Brandon in *Sense and Sensibility* ironically proves desirable to the extent of securing Elinor's future nearby. The worst outcome for Jane would probably have been separation from her sister. Better than one of them marrying and the other remaining at home was the option Jane took on 3 December 1802: to remain unmarried and together. This preference is acknowledged in Mrs Austen's phrase, they were 'wedded to each other' (Lefroy family history, quoted in Honan, 186). Gradually it was a choice they signalled to others by adopting a prematurely middle-aged style of dress.

Jane Austen's peripatetic pattern of life operated throughout George Austen's remaining years, though usually the family now came back to Bath by the end of October. Three months after settling into a new address, at 3 Green Park Buildings, George Austen died after a short illness on 21 January 1805. His loss was felt deeply, and it changed their lives. Mrs Austen, Cassandra, and Jane were caught in the familiar trap for dependent women of the professional classes when they lost the male breadwinner. It fell to James and Henry Austen to take charge of the discussions on how the brothers would contribute a sum sufficient to maintain 'the dear trio'. Mrs Austen would still have an income of £210, but that, even with Tom Fowle's legacy of £1000 for Cassandra, was insufficient. James and Henry each pledged £50 a year, which was probably difficult for both of them. Edward, as expected, gave £100. Frank stoutly offered £100, which his mother halved.

In that year Mrs Austen, Cassandra, Jane, and Martha Lloyd stayed at Worthing from mid-September to early November, and only then returned to Bath. On 2 July 1806 they left the spa town for good, and spent the rest of the summer with relatives, beginning with the Leighs of

Adlestrop. In August the Austens moved with Thomas Leigh to stay at Stoneleigh Abbey, the setting for hard negotiations concerning the will of the recently deceased Mary Leigh of Stoneleigh. In the event James Leigh-Perrot, one of the two possible heirs—both in their seventies—renounced his life interest in Stoneleigh to Thomas Leigh, in favour of a sum of £24,000 for himself, together with an annuity of £2000. Mrs Austen was severely disappointed when, after this windfall, no generous gift from the Leigh-Perrots for the three women was forthcoming. The plight of a woman denied an inheritance forms the subject of Austen's abandoned fragment of a novel, written on paper watermarked '1803' and subsequently published as *The Watsons* in the second edition of Edward Austen-Leigh's *Memoir*. The heroine, Emma Watson, expects to be the heir or at least a beneficiary of the uncle and aunt who brought her up, but her uncle leaves everything to his wife, believing that she will look after Emma. She in turn falls in love with an Irishman, implicitly an adventurer, and her money reverts to him.

Between mid-August and late September 1806 the women visited Edward Cooper and his family at Hamstall Ridware in Staffordshire, where Jane caught whooping cough from her cousins. After this they went to Steventon rectory and on 10 October, along with Frank Austen and his wife, Mary Gibson, they moved to lodgings in Southampton. In February 1807 they found a suitable house in Castle Square, which they shared for two years with Frank, Mary, and their children. Then a long-term solution was organized by Edward: he found a roomy, unpretentious house with six bedrooms in the centre of the Hampshire village of Chawton, near the large manor house that he himself owned. The Austen sisters, their mother, and Martha Lloyd moved there on 7 July 1809, and from this point Austen's career as a published writer could begin.

Austen at Chawton

A published writer

Before the end of her stay at Southampton Jane Austen was preparing for the writing she meant to return to once at Chawton. In her new home she was able to establish a routine for her own work with a minimal place in it for housework. Her nephew Edward Austen-Leigh does not comment on the marked generosity of three older women, who agreed to manage the household while Jane wrote. Instead he admired Jane's ladylike discretion in covering her work with blotting paper in order to keep her secret, that she was writing for publication, from the neighbours. This was rather like her brother Henry's disingenuous claim that she was prevailed upon with difficulty to publish.

Jane Austen dealt directly and firmly with her two publishers, Thomas Egerton and John Murray, complained when they were dilatory, and took a close interest in the progress of each of her publications, the costs of printing and paper (for which she was liable), and the copyrights and subsequent editions. She was not ashamed of meaning to make money.

Thomas Egerton, a friend of her brother Henry, had distributed James Austen's mildly satirical monthly magazine *The Loiterer* (January 1789–March 1790) in London. In the winter of 1810–11 a standard agreement was reached with him that *Sense and Sensibility* would 'be published on commission', which meant in practice that the author took a percentage of any profits, but had to bear the losses. But, though the novel duly went to press in January 1811, the printers proceeded slowly for much of the year. *Sense and Sensibility* was eventually advertised from 30 October 1811 in *The Star*, and on 31 October in the *Morning Chronicle*. Published in three volumes and priced at 15s., it probably had a print run of 1000 or fewer. It was also anonymous, with the attribution on the title-page 'By a Lady'. Still the first edition sold out, and brought Austen '£140 beside the copyright'. It was reviewed favourably in the *Critical Review* in February 1812 and in the *British Critic* in May. The former praised Austen for her 'knowledge of character' and her expert blending of 'a great deal of good sense with the lighter matter of the piece' (4th ser., 1.149). A second edition, revised by the author, was first advertised in *The Star* on 29 October 1813 at 18*s*. but sold slowly.

According to Edward Austen-Leigh's *Memoir*, *Pride and Prejudice* was also revised in 1809–10 at the same time as *Sense and Sensibility*, although cuts were still being made later. R. W. Chapman argues that the plot fits the calendars of 1811 and 1812, pointing to some major revisions, but others doubt that a significant overhaul could have occurred so late, especially if Austen was already working on *Mansfield Park* in 1811. The copyright of the novel was sold to Egerton in autumn 1812 for £110, not for the £150 that Austen wanted. She received her first published copy of *Pride and Prejudice* on 27 January 1813, saying that she had 'got my own darling Child from London' (*Letters*, 201), and on the next day it was advertised in the *Morning Chronicle* as being 'published this day', priced 18*s*. The print run is not known, but Geoffrey Keynes suggests 1500 copies. Austen could not correct mistakes in the reprinted second edition because she had lost the copyright. She declared that the book was 'rather too light & bright & sparkling', and that it required 'shade', but on the whole she was 'quite vain enough & well satisfied enough' (*Letters*, 203). Elizabeth Bennet was 'as delightful a creature as ever appeared in print, & how I shall be able to tolerate those who do not like *her* at least, I do not know' (ibid., 201). The three reviews—in the *British Critic* (21 February 1813), *Critical Review* (March 1813), and *New Review* (1 April 1813)—were favourable. Thanks to his purchase of the copyright, indeed cheap at the price, Egerton was able to print a second edition in October 1813 and a third in 1817 from which Austen was unable to profit. It was the runaway success among her publications.

The planning of *Mansfield Park*—her most ambitious novel yet, and the first to be written at Chawton—began some time before 1811, and according to Cassandra the work was finished soon after June 1813, although Jane's letters concerning *Mansfield Park* to her siblings and to Martha Lloyd were (despite Cassandra's comment) most frequent between January and September 1813. It was offered to Thomas Egerton possibly in January 1814, and Henry was reading the proof copy early in March. According to an advertisement in *The Star* it was published 'this day', 9 May 1814, priced 18*s.*, most probably with a print run of 1250 copies. By 14 November all copies were sold, and Austen's profit was at least £320—more than she received in her lifetime for any other novel.

Austen's fourth novel, *Emma*, which followed in 1816, was longer but was written rapidly in fourteen months between 21 January 1814 and 29 March 1815, according to Cassandra. Annoyed by Egerton's inattention, Austen offered *Emma* in August or September 1815 to John Murray, who on 15 October volunteered £450 for the copyright of *Emma, Mansfield Park*, and *Sense and Sensibility*. Henry Austen protested at the poor terms in November, and this time Jane Austen retained her copyrights. She met Murray, following her letter to him on 3 November: it was agreed that second editions of *Mansfield Park* and *Emma* would both be published on standard commission. On 23 November 1815 Austen complained to Murray of printer's delays, but she was soon 'soothed & complimented into tolerable comfort' (*Letters*, 298).

The reason for Murray's attentiveness could have been the news that the prince regent's librarian, James Stanier Clarke, was encouraging Austen to dedicate her next book to the prince, since he was one of her admirers. On behalf of the prince, Stanier Clarke invited Jane to visit the prince's London residence, Carlton House, and while showing her round conveyed the impression that though she was not obliged to make the dedication it would be civil and almost certainly beneficial financially to do so. She also had to pay for a bound copy for the prince. *Emma* was duly advertised in December 1815 and published later that month (though dated 1816 on the title pages). Murray printed two thousand copies of *Emma*, which proved too many. With only 1248 sold by October 1816, 539 copies were finally remaindered at 2*s.* each in 1820. One likely outcome was that *Emma* competed with John Murray's second edition of *Mansfield Park* (19 February 1816), which accordingly did not sell well, and the wholesale price was soon reduced to 11*s.* 6*d.* A shocking initial loss of £182 8*s.* 3*d.* was set against profits of *Emma* (£231 1*s.* 3*d.*), leaving Austen in her lifetime only £48 13*s.* to show for her finest novel.

Jane Austen was not only a careful businesswoman when dealing with her publishers. In relation first to Egerton and then to Murray she clearly had her own plan to produce several novels from Chawton, at least three more to match the three novels of the 1790s that her Steventon family knew. They were not to come out too fast, or they would tire the public and perhaps compete with one another, as *Emma* did with the second edition of *Mansfield*

Park. To avoid monotony, each heroine was to be a distinct personality, an individualist and flawed ('pictures of perfection' made Austen 'sick & wicked'; *Letters*, 335). Her biggest decisions, not articulated but visible in some of her fragments, novellas, and novels, were taken between 1809 and 1813. They involved an overhaul of the template from the 1790s to which *Pride and Prejudice* and *Sense and Sensibility* adhere. Those early novels, and the most depressed and bitter of her fragments, 'The Watsons', had made common cause with girls looking for legacies, as stated most forthrightly by the adolescent Margaret Dashwood: 'I wish that somebody would give us all a large fortune apiece!' (vol. 1, chap. 17). This simplistic theme allowed other authors to dwell on occasionally vulgar and usually immature characters in unappealing settings and circumstances. Austen in her mid-thirties believed she could do better, but in the meantime was content to reissue her novels of the 1790s polished and burnished but not rethought. After them she aimed at more sophisticated readers. She sought to outgrow the poor relatives' chorus.

In the novels written at Chawton Austen moved her action to large houses, alone or contrasted with other houses—first to *Mansfield Park*; next to the suburban comforts of Highbury, Surrey, in *Emma*; and then, by a backward glance in *Persuasion*, to Kellynch and a more élite, aristocratic Bath (drawing on evenings spent in the inertia of the Leigh-Perrot drawing-room). Technically this change required new models to draw into her text by way of allusion. No longer so tied to the courtship plot—with its conventional routine of a sequence of frustrating delays and near catastrophes, followed by a sudden resolution—Austen had to rethink her structure, and marginalize without quite losing novelettish incident. These two projects were strikingly achieved in *Mansfield Park* and *Emma*.

Sentiment, experience, and reflection

After *Sense and Sensibility*, Austen's next novel of sentiment was *Mansfield Park*. Here the seat of emotion appears to reside in the desire of lovers but more often lies in the sufferings of siblings and cousins. Behind the façade of a courtship novel, then, *Mansfield Park*'s originality is its base in the lives of the Steventon Austens. The slow, quiet flow of the plot into which the narrative slackens after Sir Thomas Bertram's return from the West Indies throws into relief the unnatural behaviour precipitated by the theatricals, the numerous small acts of social cowardice or treachery between brothers and sisters and cousins; even Edmund Bertram betrays Fanny Price when he fails to stand up for her against his bullying brother and sister. These points of tension, and the young people's conversations, strongly convey real-life experience. Aged about fifteen Jane's brother Edward had been adopted by a childless couple, the Knights, and spent school holidays in their big silent house at Godmersham until sent abroad in 1786. This is an experience relived by Fanny in the novel. The two youngest boys, Frank and Charles, went aged fourteen to sea in wartime, experiencing both terror and homesickness, though not much is said of this by William Price in the novel. Austen writes an eloquent passage on William's reception when at

last he comes back from the Far East to visit his
sister:

> Fanny had never known so much felicity in her life, as in this unchecked, equal, fearless intercourse with the brother and friend, who was opening all his heart to her, telling her all his hopes and fears...and with whom...all the evil and good of their earliest years could be gone over again...with the fondest recollection. An advantage this, a strengthener of love, in which even the conjugal tie is beneath the fraternal. Children of the same family, the same blood, with the same first associations and habits, have some means of enjoyment in their power, which no subsequent connections can supply. (vol. 2, chap. 6)

Fanny's meditation on family life throws light on Austen's tenderness towards her own sister and brothers. Siblings bond better in her novels than husbands with wives or parents with children.

In the early chapters of *Sense and Sensibility* Austen had openly exposed family ruptures—the unjust will of Old Francis, and the greed of a brother or sister-in-law. From reading between the lines of the letters she wrote as her books came out, it appears that Jane had to fear the reactions of some of her relatives on seeing themselves in print. Understandably, Mary Lloyd and her husband, James Austen, might have wondered if neighbours were being encouraged to see them as John and Fanny Dashwood. On the appearance of *Mansfield Park*, Austen certainly had to worry about whether the recently widowed Henry would recognize in Mary Crawford traits of his late wife, Eliza, who had died in April 1813. As herself Eliza's first cousin, her sister-in-law, and in the past her friend, Austen had to approach her character Mary Crawford with circumspection. It is Henry Crawford who is alone made fully vicious in the novel, for his cynical project of making first the Bertram sisters, then their younger cousin Fanny, love him at their peril. When Henry Austen was reading the last part of the novel, Jane wrote with apparent relief to Cassandra that their brother was mercifully unsuspicious, that is, he merely 'admires H. Crawford—I mean properly—as a clever, pleasant Man' (*Letters*, 256).

Emma probably developed as a companion piece to *Mansfield Park*: there are, at any rate, many elegant contrasts as well as variations and similarities between the two novels. Instead of a big-house interior, Austen creates most ingeniously, through many reported conversations, a large, diverse, populated village, recently swollen by an influx of suburbanites. Its scenes are set in a variety of modern-feeling drawing-rooms, in the open air, and in the street, as Highbury residents move about their business. Austen found one lever to start her plot, and a key name: in a story in the *Lady's Magazine* of 1802 called 'Guilt Pursued by Conscience', a rich Mr Knightly had married a girl of uncertain parentage from a local boarding-school. Another source was a play by the Viennese dramatist August von Kotzebue, *Die Versöhnung*, which Austen saw at Bath on 22 June 1799. Translated by Thomas Dibdin as *The Birthday*, this was a sentimental comedy about a faultless daughter, Emma Bertram, whose filial devotion to her invalid father had led her to resolve never to marry. Another play by Kotzebue, adapted for the stage by Elizabeth Inchbald as *Lovers' Vows*, featured in *Mansfield Park*.

In *Emma* Austen makes Harriet Smith a weak, almost burlesque version of the threatening strangers who enter the community in *Mansfield Park*. She is the unsuspicious simple-minded pawn of Emma Woodhouse, who unsolicited takes on the seemingly benign role of Harriet's match-maker. There are three other strangers, Jane Fairfax, Mrs Elton, and Frank Churchill. Jane seems mysterious because she is secretly engaged to Frank. The mystery tempts Emma and the irresponsible Frank to invent a novelettish romance for Jane. Mrs Elton has ambitions to lead Highbury society and worms her way into organizing or projecting Highbury entertainments at other people's expense. From Yorkshire, Mrs Churchill, a domineering woman who is never seen, controls the comings and goings of the essentially weak Frank Churchill.

The most striking contrast between Austen's two more innovative novels seems at first sight to lie in the personality of the heroine: Fanny Price, so long shy and apparently uncertain, is succeeded by Emma Woodhouse, energetic and over-confident. Emma is seen at her best as an adult within a trio of observing adults, the others being her erstwhile governess and mother figure, Mrs Weston, and her future husband, Knightley. The conversations between the three seem supremely natural, uncensorious, understanding, mature, as if based on the virtues Austen observed in the people she lived with and best respected, or could confidently claim in herself. Emma as an 'imaginist' expresses Austen's own creative exuberance and her vocational interest in character and plot. But a central impulse behind the treatment of Emma is an unsparing confrontation with faults others saw in Jane Austen, such as impatience, refusal to suffer fools, and a sense of her own superiority, not of rank but of talent. Certainly her family would have conceded that Jane, like Emma, had a dutiful regard for the parish's old ladies. On the other hand Cassandra especially would have seen—and Jane lets her readers see—in Emma's affront to Miss Bates, the licence Jane permitted herself in the privacy of letters, of making jokes about her neighbours, some of them unkind. She found one such target in the Revd Henry Hall of Monk Sherborne, Hampshire, whose wife 'was brought to bed yesterday of a dead child, some weeks before she expected, oweing to a fright.— I suppose she happened unawares to look at her husband' (*Letters*, 17). Certainly on occasions she could be offensive.

By 1813 Austen apparently knew that there would be at least three more novels after the publication of *Pride and Prejudice*. The third is *Persuasion*. Writing began on 8 August 1815, and a first draft was completed by 18 July 1816. It too develops variations on established themes which contemporary readers of novels would be expected to recognize. A romantic plot is triggered by the arrival of a familiar man and former fiancé, Captain Wentworth, who resembles the gallant Captain Walsingham in *Manoeuvring* (1809), a domestic comedy by Maria Edgeworth, then the

regarded highly. In 1814 she wrote to her neice
Anna Lefroy: 'I have made up my mind to like
no Novels really, but Miss Edgeworth's, Yours &
my own' (*Letters*, 278). Each of Austen's six published novels, except *Pride and Prejudice*, borrows
somewhere from Edgeworth. Thus in *Persuasion*,
Wentworth's simultaneous courtship of two Musgrove sisters echoes behaviour resented in Edgeworth's *Vivian* (1812), while Louisa Musgrove's
mistimed leap into Wentworth's arms on the Cobb
at Lyme Regis mirrors in *Vivian* the tumble of the
hoydenish Lady Julia into the sea at Plymouth (in
later editions, Yarmouth).

Quietly and wittily allusive, *Persuasion* is the
most elegant of courtship novels, a reflection on
romantic love and marriage for men and women,
whether in late adolescence or nearing middle
age. Anne Elliot has experienced eight years
earlier a romance that was broken off, thanks to
the disapproval of her father and the negative
advice of Lady Russell. Since then she has refused
an offer of marriage from a neighbour, Charles

Musgrove, after which Charles marries her less appealing sister Mary. The action opens on Anne in her loveless home, Kellynch Hall, living with her cold and snobbish father and elder sister, who neglect her. When these two leave for Bath she moves to Uppercross, where she can reflect on what her life would have been had she married Charles Musgrove: a warmer, noisier, child-ridden, unstimulating existence, the men obsessed with field sports, everyone's days and evenings spent in a crowd. Jane's own brothers, and two of the sons of her brother Edward Knight, were keen on field sports. The sequential settings in *Persuasion* review the noise and weariness of married life with realism and not much sign of regret. None of the households with children described by Austen seems positively attractive. Only Mrs Croft associates her marriage with energy and adventure, and she is not at home, but with her husband, the admiral, when he goes to sea. The reminiscences, somewhat idealized, are those of Frank Austen's wife, Mary Gibson.

Austen's swerve into romance as she grew older had little to do with the sentimentalism of the 1790s, and more with close observation and reflection. She had told her motherless niece Fanny Knight that her age, twenty-one, was the time to form a deep and permanent attachment—a true marriage. But in the same letter Austen had 'no scruple in saying' that Fanny 'cannot be in Love' with her suitor John Plumptre (*Letters*, 279), advice that proved as decisive for Fanny as Lady Russell's for Anne at nineteen, though Fanny persevered, to marry Sir Edward Knatchbull in October 1820. *Persuasion* offers a full complement of experienced older women. It has mother figures for nearly adult daughters; adult daughters entering the years when marriage has become unlikely; and, in the novel's present time but also in women's memories, the experience of being eighteen and of falling in love. In *Persuasion* the tally of good marriages is small indeed, and is confined to sailors: Admiral and Mrs Croft (the older generation, and now cheerful and prosperous) and Captain and Mrs Harville (hardworked and selfless parents of young children, in cramped accommodation). At first meeting, the literary Captain Benwick seems an arch-romantic: he has loved and been loved by an exceptional woman, Fanny Harville, who has died; and he is as ardent a lover of poetry as Willoughby and Marianne. But Benwick makes what looks like a poor choice by engaging himself to the very ordinary Louisa Musgrove, merely because she fell in his way during the short time in which she is vulnerable, passive, and pale, like a fictional heroine. Louisa and Henrietta Musgrove still regret, and rightly, that their brother Charles is not married to Anne Elliot. Mrs Smith has married the man of her choice, to suffer thereafter because, being spend-thrift, weak, and a poor judge of men, he left his property in the hands of the treacherous William Walter Elliot. The last-named is a marital adven-turer, in the past supposedly after Elizabeth Elliot, currently in pursuit of Anne. His next liaison with the equally unscrupulous Mrs Clay is not so much a marriage as a business deal.

Against this panorama of lost illusions or duplicity, mercenariness and betrayal, the gentle but steady

courtship of mature lovers is very moving, especially in the rewritten and brilliantly contrived
proposal scene at the White Hart. In the conversation regarding Benwick between Anne and
Captain Harville about male and female fidelity
there is a compacted world of Austen's own family
experience, and one of the strongest insights anywhere in her writing into the novelist's sym-
pathy with her sister Cassandra. In an undertone
Anne describes Cassandra's fidelity, 'that of loving
longest, when existence or when hope is lost' (vol.
2, chap. 11).

Death and image

Austen's last year

After completing *Persuasion* in August 1816, Jane
Austen wrote a preface for *Northanger Abbey*,
describing the previous attempt to publish. Henry
had bought back the original manuscript of
'Susan'—now renamed 'Catherine'—from Benjamin Crosby that year. But Austen again put it
aside: 'Miss Catherine is put upon the Shelve for
the present, and I do not know that she will ever
come out' (*Letters*, 333). She had suffered back
pain during the summer of 1816, and that autumn
fell ill with a variety of symptoms: nausea, diar-
rhoea, muscle weakness, and fatigue. Modern
medical expertise suggests tuberculosis (of the
lungs or stomach) or cancer (of the stomach or

bowel). The increased pigmentation of her skin, however, is now regarded as a sign of Addison's disease, and the result of the malfunction of the cortex of the adrenal glands. Good doctors were tried in succession, but there was no cure.

Austen could barely write that autumn. To Cassandra, on 8 September, she wondered that Jane West could 'have written such Books & collected so many hard words' because 'Composition seems to me Impossible, with a head full of Joints of Mutton & doses of rhubarb' (*Letters*, 321). She did, however, pick up a new project, *Sanditon*, in January 1817. Impressively she stuck to her grand plan for her Chawton novels, always to surprise her readers by using a different format from that of the previous novel, or in this case to try a burlesque format newer than *Northanger Abbey*. The setting is a south-coast seaside village in a state of headlong development. Through the pleasant and sensible Charlotte Heywood the reader encounters one by one the eccentrics who have taken the place over: hypochondriacs (this term then connoted the social maladies of the idle rich) such as three members of the Parker family; entrepreneurs, managers, and advertisers, such as the senior Mr Parker, who once lived in a pleasant, undeveloped house and estate, in a sheltered position; and Lady Denham, a woman of power and authority. A rich widow who has survived two rich husbands, she is a female version of Austen's great-uncle Francis, and like him surrounded by a court of acquisitive nieces and nephews. One of these is a literary poseur, Sir Edward Denham, who models himself on Samuel Richardson's Lovelace, and aspires to seduce Clara Brereton, the novel's nearest approximation to the heroine of melo-drama. This is a tough, cynical study of greed, meanness, and 'hypochondria'. It would have been hard in the best circumstances to sustain and finish. Jane Austen lacked the time, and set the tale aside for good on 18 March 1817. Edited by R. W. Chapman, the manuscript was published as *Fragments of a Novel by Jane Austen* in 1925.

It was a dreadful winter and spring for other reasons. Henry Austen, like other receivers-general of taxes, had the use of tax money between collection and remission. This customary practice came under severe criticism as the post-war financial crisis deepened. Henry Austen was already pronounced bankrupt on 15 March 1816. His guarantors for the receivership, James Leigh-Perrot (£10,000) and Edward Knight (£20,000), both lost their sureties, and when Edward in particular got into difficulties, the Steventon Austens were faced with losing their home. Other family members—Frank and Charles—lost lesser sums. Even Henry's servants had banked with him, and their losses were irreparable. Jane Austen, in the unwitnessed will she wrote on 27 April 1817 making Cassandra her executor, thoughtfully left £50 each for Henry and for his housekeeper Mme Bigeon.

As the weather grew warmer, Austen claimed to be slowly gathering strength. But her symptoms persisted, and in May the family agreed she should have the best possible advice—from Giles King Lyford, a surgeon at the county hospital in Winchester. Her last weeks in Winchester witnessed more short rallies, in which she felt alert, even creative. On 13 June, however, Charles found her 'very ill', and Lyford told the family that her case was desperate. On St Swithin's day, 15 July, she composed a comic poem, a curse addressed by the saint to the people of Winchester (Latin name 'Venta'):

> Oh! subjects rebellious! Oh Venta depraved!
> When once we are buried you think we are dead
> But behold me immortal ...

Her pain returned on the evening of 17 July, as Lyford warned it would. Cassandra asked if she wanted anything, to which Jane replied, typically, with a quotation, in this case from *Pilgrim's Progress*, 'nothing but death'. She died at 8 College Street, Winchester, at 4.30 a.m. on 18 July, Cassandra beside her. Her funeral was held in Winchester Cathedral at 8 a.m. on 24 July 1817. The mourners were her brothers Edward, Henry, and Frank, with James, who was also ill, represented by his son Edward.

Portraits

Only two authentic images of Jane Austen are known to exist, both sketches with watercolour by Cassandra. The earliest, dated 1804 and initialled 'C.E.A.', is a rear view which depicts Austen sitting out of doors wearing a blue dress and a large bonnet which comically obscures her face and head. The second sketch (*c*.1810, National Portrait Gallery, London) is the only certain and authentic representation of Jane's face: a mature woman, she is looking away to her right, her dark brown curls escaping from a lace cap. The family had reservations about this image, which had a pursed mouth suggesting secrecy and perhaps anger; Anna Austen (Mrs Lefroy) called it 'so hideously unlike' (Le Faye, *Family Record*, 280). In 1869 Edward Austen-Leigh commissioned a softer and more rounded version from a local artist, James Andrews of Maidenhead; however, the same idealization recurred and Cassandra's Jane became, in Margaret Anne Doody's words, 'sweet-faced, big-eyed, placid . . . the image of the perfect sister and aunt'. An engraving by Lizars of Andrews's watercolour was used in 1870 as the frontispiece to Austen-Leigh's *Memoir*; this too was criticized by Anna's half-sister Caroline for the treatment of Jane's eyes—Cassandra had made them too large, round, and naïve.

In addition to Cassandra's two sketches there are three further portraits which, though at times identified as Jane, cannot be claimed as authentic likenesses. Two are silhouettes. The first, entitled *L'aimable Jane*, is now also owned by the National Portrait Gallery. It was found in a copy of the second edition of *Mansfield Park* (1816), pasted to the rear endpaper of volume 2, and is thought possibly to be by a Mrs Collins, an artist working in Bath about 1800. The second silhouette, owned by Winchester Cathedral Library, has been claimed on the basis of its inscription to be the work of Austen herself, dated 1815. The style, however, suggests a much later work of about 1895. A third purported likeness is a watercolour sketch of a woman wearing a large black feathered hat, which occurs in an album compiled between 1791 and 1804 by James Stanier Clarke, the librarian to the prince of Wales. The untitled and undated sketch depicts a youthful woman whose extravagant dress and hat are at odds with the taste of the year 1815 when Austen, at forty, visited Stanier Clarke at Carlton House.

A further portrait has proved less easy to dismiss as a likeness of Jane Austen, though, equally, there is no conclusive evidence that it is an image of the novelist. This is the so-called Rice portrait. A professional studio painting, it depicts a brown-haired girl aged between thirteen and fifteen. The girl's hair is neatly shaped to her head, the texture healthy and glossy. The eyes are brown and rather narrow, the skin typically brunette but perhaps powdered, the nose straight, the mouth small.

Doubt over the sitter's identity has focused debate on differing opinions as to the date of the painting. What has been agreed retrospectively is that in the late 1810s the portrait was in the possession of the Motley Austens of Kippington, Jane Austen's cousins and descendants of her great uncle 'Old Francis' Austen. In 1817 the Kippington estate passed to Colonel Thomas Austen, the second son of Francis Motley Austen (*d*. 1815) and his wife, Elizabeth, *née* Wilson. Probably in 1818, Thomas gave the portrait to his friend Thomas Harding Newman of Nelmes, Essex, and his wife-to-be, Eliza Hall, who became its legal owner. The Harding Newman family believed the portrait to be the work of Johan Zoffany (a description that might be contemporary shorthand for a family picture) and to portray the young Jane Austen. With the death of Harding Newman in 1856 the portrait passed to his son, and Eliza's stepson, also Thomas. In December 1880 the younger Thomas wrote to his friend J. R. Bloxham about the painting, giving certain details that could have come only from a Kippington source:

I should like to give [a] painting, of Jane Austen the novelist by Zoffany to her relative, your neighbour Morland Rice. It is of a girl about fifteen & came into my family, the gift of Col. Austen of Chippington [Kippington] to my ... stepmother; my father's second wife, who was a great admirer of the novelist. I can remember Colonel Austen visiting this place.

DEATH AND IMAGE

The younger Thomas Harding Newman subsequently bequeathed the painting to his friend John Morland Rice, whom he knew to be a collateral descendant of Jane Austen. The portrait was first published in the 1884 edition of *The Letters of Jane Austen* edited by Morland Rice's cousin Lord Brabourne. It remains in the possession of the Rice family, who argue that the painting is of Austen and dates from the late 1780s.

Scholarly debate over the sitter's identity arose in the twentieth century. Questions were first raised during the 1930s when the National Portrait Gallery concluded that the painting—which is undated, untitled, and has no discernible signature—was not by Zoffany but more likely the work of Ozias Humphry. Moreover, it was argued that the child's dress and the painting style dated the picture after 1800, and possibly as late as 1810, and therefore that it could not be of Austen. A more general reason for doubt is the absence of first-hand contemporary evidence about the portrait. Who saw it or knew of its existence in the immediate family circle, from Jane's adolescence and after? Who commissioned the portrait and where was it in Austen's lifetime? The suggestion of a later dating was reiterated in the 1990s, notably by Deirdre Le Faye who argues that the portrait is probably by Matthew William Peters, and the sitter not Jane Austen but Colonel Thomas Austen's niece Mary Anne Campion (1797–1825).

None the less the girl's identity remains contested. An alternative interpretation dates the Rice portrait to the late 1780s or early 1790s, with the possibility that it depicts Austen aged between thirteen and fifteen. The suggested provenance is that the portrait was commissioned from Ozias Humphry by Old Francis shortly after the Steventon Austens' visit to Kippington in 1788. Thomas Austen, who later gave the portrait away, is known to have met Jane during this visit. A letter from Henry Morland Rice in 1884 included a statement from Fanny Caroline Lefroy, the daughter of Anna, that the portrait dates from 1788 or 1789 and was of the novelist aged thirteen.

More recent research has questioned Lefroy's precise dating, but maintains that—if interpreted as a whole, and seen in the context of the period—the Rice portrait is still best identified as an eighteenth-century work. Evidence for dating items of costume is often inconclusive. It is especially difficult to show that a type of high-waisted dress that was brought into fashion in France by Marie Antoinette in the 1780s could not have occurred contemporaneously in the variant seen in the Rice portrait. At the same time the girl's short, straight hair suggests a style fashionable in the early years of the French Revolution, while her parasol accords with an accessory popular from the 1780s. The influence of Thomas Gainsborough (1727–1788) can be discerned in the girl's emergence from a dark background which surrounds her head. It is also plausible to see in the spirited figure something of the lively and comically gifted Austen whom Humphry would have got to know during the initial sittings. Finally, the late twentieth-century discovery of Austen family wills and papers shows Old Francis to have been among the 'new men' who set up a dynasty in accordance with the effective system of estate law known as strict settlement. This restricted the owner's expenditure by limiting it to a single life as owner, and placed items of value in trust. Old Francis's interest in strict settlement demonstrates his wish to advance the Austens' standing, an act for which the commissioning of family portraits, both as cultural artefacts and investments, was wholly appropriate. A portrait capturing the youth and innocence of his great-niece Jane would have been an obvious contribution to this end. The existence of strict settlement also ensured that portraits commissioned or already owned by Francis, along with all moveable objects of value, would have been held in trust from 1796 when the Motley Austens moved in.

Weighing the arguments for and against, the identity of the girl in the Rice portrait remains unknown and, possibly, unknowable. The painting, however, continues to prompt interesting questions. What does it tell us about the workings of the much-vaunted estate system?

What might it tell us about relations within the Austen family at this time? Did Eliza Hall, the painting's recipient in 1818 and a firm admirer of the novelist, really know the portrait to be of Jane Austen?

Austen's reputation

Early recollections and criticism

Persuasion and *Northanger Abbey* were published together in four volumes by John Murray, prefaced by Henry Austen's 'Biographical notice of the author' (dated 13 December 1817), the first acknowledgement in print of Jane Austen as the author of her six novels. The publication was organized by Henry and Cassandra, but the decision to pair the youthful, satirical *Northanger Abbey* with the mature, autumnal *Persuasion* was probably Jane Austen's, since it matched her steady practice, by then, of pairing her novels so that the reader saw in them both similarity and contrast. The setting is the same—Bath—but the subtlety and sentiment of *Persuasion* are offset by the sophisticated naïvety of *Northanger Abbey*. 1750 copies were printed in December 1817. The work was advertised in mid- to late December and appeared late in the month, with '1818' on the title-page. Prompt reviews appeared in the *British Critic* (March 1818) and in the *Edinburgh Magazine* and *Literary Miscellany* (May 1818). Initial sales were rapid: the dual publication earned £518 6s. 5d. Jan Fergus calculates Austen's overall literary earnings, including copyrights, to have been at least £1625, most of it received after her death. In her lifetime she received something over £631, perhaps as much as £668. It was insufficient for her to support herself by writing.

The reception of Jane Austen's novels has always had a private and a public dimension. Her novels were published anonymously: only a favoured few in her immediate family circle knew of the publication of *Sense and Sensibility* (1811) and *Pride and Prejudice* (1813). But in spring and summer 1813 her brother Henry Austen gossiped tirelessly to his friends and acquaintances of his sister's novels, which publicized her work and encouraged his upper-class circles to spread her fame further. The care with which Jane Austen kept the comments on *Mansfield Park* and *Emma* sent to her by some of these friends clearly indicates that, though she had initially wanted to remain anonymous, she enjoyed her public favour as well as her sales.

Because of her anonymity Austen initially received relatively few reviews. The only notable published review article of her lifetime was one by Walter Scott (as usual unsigned) in the prestigious *Quarterly Review* (vol. 14, dated October 1815, published March 1816, 188–201). While his topic was purportedly *Emma* (1816), Scott offered an overview of Austen's publications so far, from which, to her irritation, he accidentally omitted *Mansfield Park*. This was nevertheless to take her seriously, and indeed Scott was plainly prepared to make claims for Austen's importance to the English novel. He even suggests that the 'romance', a Gothic and historical fashion launched in the 1790s by himself and others, was now superseded by novels of ordinary life, village and domestic, with Maria Edgeworth and Jane Austen as its most skilful practitioners. This appears generous and self-effacing, but Scott undercuts his flattery before he is through. He cannot help hinting at the colourfulness of his own fictional world, peopled with 'robbers, smugglers, bailiffs, dungeons and mad-houses' (192). Even Edgeworth sounds relatively lively—'the scenes of Miss E are laid in higher life, varied by more romantic incident, and by her remarkable power of embodying and illustrating national character' (193). Austen's speciality is by contrast to remain faithful to 'the middling classes of society' in southern England and to 'the art of copying from nature … in the common walks of life'—or 'presenting to the reader, instead of the splendid scenes of an imaginary world, a correct and striking representation of that which is daily taking place around him' (193). It is correct then. And it is parochial. These words would be used as reproaches to Austen later in the nineteenth century.

Austen's effusive brother Henry proved another dubious ally. His eight-page 'Biographical notice' prefacing the posthumous edition of *Northanger*

Abbey and *Persuasion* (1818) was written in the flush of his new evangelicalism, and unabashedly idealized Austen as a daughter and sister who led an almost wholly private life. 'A life of usefulness, literature, and religion, was not by any means a life of event'. At home she never met reproof or 'an abatement of good-will'. She was modest and retiring:

> An invincible distrust of her own judgment induced her to withhold her works from the public...She could scarcely believe what she termed her great good fortune when *Sense and Sensibility* produced a clear profit of about £150. Few so gifted were so truly unpretending. She regarded the above sum as a prodigious recompense for that which had cost her nothing.

Her 'personal attractions' were considerable too, 'her stature was that of true elegance', her 'complexion was of the finest texture'.

Henry's unqualified praise was wearisome, and on points of detail the Austen family, at least, knew that he went too far. Cassandra, the main recipient of her sister's letters, could not have said 'she never uttered a hasty, a silly or a severe expression', or 'Faultless herself, as nearly as human nature can be, she always sought, in the faults of others, something to excuse, to forgive or forget.' Another claim embarrassed the next generation of the family: 'The style of her familiar correspondence was in all respects the same as that of her novels...she never dispatched a note or letter unworthy of publication.' This misleading sentence kept up the pressure for her private letters to be published, and was partly responsible for the disappointment widely felt when in 1932 R. W. Chapman published the first substantial edition of Austen's letters. H. W. Garrod was perhaps the most outspoken critic: 'a desert of trivialities punctuated by occasional oases of clever malice' ('Jane Austen: a depreciation', *Transactions of the Royal Society of Literature*, new ser., 8, 1928, 23).

Henry went on to inflate the extent and seriousness of Austen's reading, and to omit her familiarity with humour, burlesque, caricature, and stage farce, not to speak of woman-centred magazine fiction aimed at the lower end of the market. One of the few quotations from Jane and the very best moment in Henry's eulogy was lifted from a letter she wrote to her novel-writing nephew Edward when she was already seriously ill in late 1816. It is her description of the difference between her style and method and his: 'How could I possibly join them on to the little bit (two Inches wide) of Ivory on which I work with so fine a Brush, as produces little effect after much labour?' (*Letters*, 323). A more complex legacy left by Henry Austen was his finale, solemnly introduced: 'One trait only remains ... she was thoroughly reli-gious and devout; fearful of giving offence to God, and incapable of feeling it towards any fellow creature. On serious subjects well-instructed, both by reading and meditation'. Jane's stoical and quiet death rounds off the intended impression, of a virtuous and private woman who died resigned and grateful with her lot in life.

The review by Scott and the obituary by Henry figure repeatedly in Jane Austen's nineteenth-century reception, beginning with Richard

Whately, the future archbishop of Dublin, and reviewer for the *Quarterly Review* in January 1821 of Austen's posthumous novels. His piece was much longer and probably more important for her reputation than the pieces by Walter Scott or Henry Austen. Whately praised Austen for her domestic Christian values in contrast to those of other writers, most pointedly Maria Edgeworth: 'Miss Austen has the merit (in our judgment most essential) of being evidently a Christian writer: a merit which is much enhanced, both on the score of good taste and of practical utility, by her religion being not at all obtrusive'. There is also an observant and perceptive paragraph on Fanny Price's ability to resist the overtures of Henry Crawford in *Mansfield Park*:

> Fanny...is armed against Mr Crawford by a stronger feeling than even her disapprobation; by a vehement attachment to Edmund. The silence in which this passion is cherished—the slender hopes and enjoyments by which it is fed—the restlessness and jealousy with which it fills a mind naturally active, contented and

unsuspicious—the manner in which it tinges every event and every reflection, are painted with a vividness and a detail of which we can scarcely conceive any one but a female, and we should almost add, a female writing from recollection, capable. (*Quarterly Review*, vol. 24, January 1821, 359, 366–7)

Private readers had enjoyed Austen's work in her own lifetime, and others continued to do so throughout the nineteenth century, with all six of the novels available in new and affordable editions from the early 1830s. The vein of criticism that buoyed her reputation was the claim already voiced by Whately, and after him Thomas Babington Macaulay, that she was a 'prose Shakespeare': a masterly portrayer of character. At the same time, owing partly to Scott's ambivalence, Austen's meticulous treatment of the ordinary exposed her to a steady stream of criticism from, for example, the many Romantic writers, including almost all the major poets, who strove to transcend the commonplace and literal in their quests for idealism, the sublime, imagination, passionate love, or a form of Christianity more spiritual than Austen's late eighteenth-century Anglicanism. The Romantic reproach levelled at Austen was the simple issue of her scale—her ordinariness was also littleness, an acceptance of constraint and the mediocre, however exquisite her technique and taste. Charlotte Brontë told G. H. Lewes it was certainly so: 'an accurate daguerreotyped portrait of a common-place face; a carefully-fenced, highly cultivated garden...Miss Austen, being as you say without "sentiment", without *poetry*, may be—*is* sensible, real (more *real* than *true*), but she cannot be great' (12 and 18 January 1848, in *The Letters of Charlotte Brontë*, vol. 2, 1848–1851, ed. M. Smith, 2000, 10, 14).

Late-Victorian appreciation

Reactions to Austen's achievement varied with the disposition of the reader. Thomas Carlyle intemperately dismissed her work as 'dishwashings'. Slowly the more thoughtful male admirers of her technique, beginning with Macaulay and G. H. Lewes, introduced arguments that widened her range. Lewes especially returned to the comparison with Shakespeare, and went on the offensive against Scott's champions by describing her 'marvellous dramatic power' and the objectivity with which she presents her characters and their relationships ('The novels of Jane Austen', *Blackwood's Edinburgh Magazine*, vol. 86, July 1859, 99–113). His insight and good sense prepared the way for the most perceptive essay on Austen so far, that of Richard Simpson, a Roman Catholic friend of John Henry Newman and a Shakespearian scholar, who broke clean out of the reproach of narrowness by presenting both her humour and her irony as the techniques of a social critic rather than a miniaturist. Simpson's essay, for the *North British Review* (April 1870), considered Edward Austen-Leigh's *Memoir* (1870) a more elegant and judicious biography than Henry Austen's 'Biographical notice' half a century earlier. Margaret Oliphant's review in *Blackwood's Edinburgh Magazine* (March 1870) also made a difference by giving Jane Austen a mind of her own, a task in which Edward Austen-Leigh had failed:

Mr Austen Leigh, without meaning it, throws out of his dim little lantern a passing gleam of light upon the fine vein of feminine cynicism which pervades his aunt's mind. It is something altogether different from the rude and brutal male quality that bears the same name.... She is not surprised or offended, much less horror-stricken or indignant, when her people show vulgar or mean traits of character,... or even when they fall into those social cruelties which selfish and stupid people are so often guilty of, not without intention, but yet without the power of realising half the pain they inflict. She stands by and looks on, and gives a soft half-smile, and tells the story with an exquisite sense of its ridiculous side, and fine stinging yet soft-voiced contempt for the actors in it.... The position of mind is essentially feminine... It is the natural result of the constant though probably quite unconscious observation in which a young woman, with no active pursuit to occupy her, spends, without knowing it, so much of her time and youth. (*Blackwood's Edinburgh Magazine*, vol. 107, March 1870, 294)

At this time and in the twentieth century it was Simpson's essay that was more admired. Oliphant, however, captured more acutely than any predecessor 'the fine vein of feminine cynicism' which bonds Austen to her female readers, while she matches and to some extent subverts Simpson's confident reading of her humour and irony.

Edward Austen-Leigh's *Memoir* had one obvious advantage: it was written by someone who had grown up from 1801 in Steventon rectory, after George and Cassandra moved with their daughters to Bath in May of that year. Edward re-created life at Steventon rectory, though it is more the world of his own childhood, in a much smaller family group, than that of Jane Austen's. There should have been a second advantage. From 1813 Edward and his sisters Anna and Caroline showed their aunt their own first attempts to write, and received in return some of her most valuable letters concerning her craft. Yet Edward unaccountably fails to quote in the *Memoir* from the letters she sent him, even the great comparison of his manner with her own 'painting on ivory'. With misplaced modesty, he says nothing of how he felt when he read her advice to him as an apprentice novelist. His tribute to her is well meant, but formal, and he denies himself what the book most needs, the sound of her voice: ' "Aunt Jane" was the delight of all her nephews and nieces. We did not think of her as being clever, still less as being famous; but we valued her as one always kind, sympathising, and amusing' (Austen-Leigh, *Memoir*, chap. 1). His sisters were more demanding and specific in their comments, yet they too seemed to be under an injunction not to go into detail about their relationships with their aunt. Anna, in her regrettably brief 'Recollections of Aunt Jane' (1864), observes shrewdly that Jane was *not* the preferred aunt in Kent, *not* 'loved' by those conventionally reared nieces and nephews, who preferred the more matter-of-fact, reliable Cassandra. The Godmersham girls, beginning with the eldest, Fanny, were fully aware of the reservations their mother, Elizabeth Bridges, felt regarding Jane's cleverness. As Anna commented sourly, 'a little talent went a long way

Modern criticism, scholarship, and pleasure

Despite its omissions Austen-Leigh's *Memoir* was a stimulus to Austen criticism, and his enlarged second edition—which reproduced for the first time examples of the juvenilia, the fragment *The Watsons*, and *Lady Susan* in its entirety—opened the floodgates to other publications, initially by the family, of the letters and the remaining literary papers. 'Women of letters' were now part of the literary scene, and Austen became what she has since remained, a major writer as popular and accessible to the public as any contemporary. There have also been symptoms of resistance to her pre-eminence. Two sophisticated women writers of the earlier twentieth century, Virginia Woolf and Katherine Mansfield, expressed their reservations about 'Janeites' (a term apparently coined by George Saintsbury in 1894 in his preface to *Pride and Prejudice*). Even E. M. Forster, who confessed to being himself a Janeite, was embarrassed by the term ('Jane, how shall we ever recollect . . .', *The Nation and The Athenaeum*, 5 January 1924). Meanwhile in America, where Austen had not hitherto enjoyed so steady a readership as in Britain, major male writers expressed their decided hostility to the cult they saw gathering strength in Britain: in roughly the same period a wave of male misogyny on both sides of the Atlantic led to an intemperate assault by Mark Twain ('When I take up *Pride and Prejudice* and *Sense and Sensibility* I feel like a barkeeper entering the Kingdom of Heaven') and, less predictably, Henry James's cutting denigration of what had hitherto seemed unassailable, Austen's art:

> The tide [of her fame] has risen rather higher, I think, than the high-water mark, the highest, of her intrinsic merit and interest . . . we are dealing here in some degree . . . [with] the swift breeze of the commercial . . . I cannot help seeing her, a good deal, in the same lucky box as the Brontës . . . a case of popularity . . . a

beguiled infatuation, a sentimentalized vision.
('The lesson of Balzac', 1905, in *The House of Fiction*, 1957, 62–3)

Early to mid-twentieth-century scholars were more sympathetic. Now that classic novels of sufficient seriousness were subjects for study in schools and university, the most thoughtful of the Victorians, Richard Simpson, had important successors in another Shakespearian, A. C. Bradley (*Essays and Studies*, 1911), and a brilliant man of letters, Reginald Farrer (*Quarterly Review*, July 1917). That most useful compilation by W. and R. A. Austen-Leigh, *Jane Austen, her Life and Letters* (1913), added substantially to the materials available. They were followed from the 1920s by the steady flow of R. W. Chapman's editions from Oxford University Press: first the six novels (1923), then the *Minor Works*, containing the unfinished works and the juvenilia (between 1925 and 1951), and the *Letters* (1932). Elizabeth Jenkins wrote an accessible life of Austen in 1938. In 1939 Mary Lascelles published *Jane Austen and her Art*, the first book-length study that was a work both of modern scholarship and of literary criticism and a book that has retained its value for both academic and general readers.

The 1950s was the first decade in which more academic commentary on Austen emerged from the United States than from Britain. In 1963 a British scholar working in America, Ian Watt, edited a collection of recent articles on Austen by scholars from both sides of the Atlantic in the paperback series 'Twentieth-Century Views'. Watt's selection was fresh, creative, thought-provoking, and analytical; after the limited scope of nineteenth-century Austen criticism, it offered Austen's readers an invigorating range of new per-spectives, from Marxist and Freudian interpre-tations of single novels to influential discussions by leading scholars and philosophers of her use of irony. Without too much exaggeration, Watt in his introduction claimed that the 1950s was the decade in which the sociological combined with the 'New Critical' interest, and in which 'the main literary problems raised by the novels have at last been systematically investigated' (12). Watt picks out for special mention Lionel Trilling's famous essay on *Mansfield Park* (*Encounter*, September 1954) which after more than fifty years still retains its aura, as a deep critical engagement with ethics and duty relating Austen's novels to profound conflicts innate in Western civilization as well as the individual moral life.

Later in the twentieth century, as women's and feminist studies challenged and to a considerable extent re-routed the priority formerly given to male writers, Austen was for the first time perceived as part of a wave of late eighteenth-century female writers who addressed a growing readership of women. In the 1790s authors such as Elizabeth Inchbald, Charlotte Smith, and Mary Wollstonecraft were already using the conventions of the popular courtship romance to criticize the legal and economic barriers that society erected against women. Though averse to entering London or Bath literary circles, Austen from her schooldays actively availed herself of structures—reviews, magazines, and circulating libraries—that could disseminate the productions of the book trade through the countryside as well as the town. As a reader she disliked 'preaching', and as a writer she kept close to the conventions of comedy—witty, satirical, and sentimental— as practised in the theatre of her day. She cleverly varied the style of her heroines, yet made each of them, including even Catherine Morland, loyal and eventually self-reliant. By her frequent cross-references to other women-centred plays and novels, Austen was fully part of the stimulating conversation conducted by the literate women of her day. These advances in textual scholarship and in the understanding of Austen's literary and historical context, are now fully reflected in the nine-volume *Cambridge Edition of the Works of Jane Austen* (general editor, Janet Todd, 2005–6).

Jane Austen emerged between 1870 and 1960 as a social critic, a moralist, an incomparable artist, and latterly a popular and universal writer. Today her novels are firm favourites among book buyers and library users and feature prominently in polls of best-loved fiction, with a special attachment to *Pride and Prejudice*. It was the relatively recent recognition of Austen's universality that drove the rapid growth in the 1990s of hotly competing television and film adaptations of all six of Austen's finished novels. 1995 was a particularly notable year with an ambitious, well-cast, and conscientiously researched *Pride and Prejudice* made for television, with running time of five hours, produced by Sue Birtwistle and scripted by Andrew Davies, a team that had already succeeded with George Eliot's *Middlemarch* the preceding year. The production was deliberately literary, and committed to delivering the inward interest and complex relationships of nineteenth-century novels. In the same year Ang Lee directed a stylish and scenic *Sense and Sensibility*, scripted by Emma Thompson, an aesthetic and box-office success. Douglas McGrath's *Emma* (1996) and Patricia Rozema's *Mansfield Park* (1999) followed, both of them combining some decided merits with questionable features. Since *Emma* is very long and has many peripheral characters, the story was heavily cut for the film, which became a vehicle for Gwyneth Paltrow. The opposite fate befell *Mansfield Park*. Its heroine, Fanny Price, was made unrecognizable, by the imposition of sour traits originating in Austen's letters, mingled with the rebelliousness of a modern teenager; Sir Thomas Bertram became a slave-driver with psychopathic tendencies. 2007 again saw remarkable interest in screen adaptations of Austen, with television versions of *Mansfield Park*, *Persuasion*, and *Northanger Abbey*. Amy Heckerling's *Clueless* (1995) may have also set a trend whereby, as with some of Shakespeare's plays, the plot is retained but the setting ingeniously transferred. Inspired by *Emma* but set in a Californian high school, it has a cult following that few other Austen films command—a fitting testimony to Jane Austen's remarkable and enduring appeal.

Sources

Austen's works and letters

The Cambridge edition of the works of Jane Austen, general editor, J. Todd, 9 vols. (2005–6) · *The novels of Jane Austen: the text based on collation of the early editions,* ed. R. W. Chapman, 5 vols. (1923) · *Jane Austen: the works,* ed. R. W. Chapman, 6: *Minor works* (1954) · *'Catharine' and other writings,* ed. M. A. Doody and D. Murray (1993) · J. Modert, ed., *Jane Austen's manuscript letters in facsimile* (1989) · *Jane Austen's letters,* ed. D. Le Faye, 3rd edn (1995)

Memoirs and biographies

H. Austen, 'Biographical notice', in J. Austen, *Northanger Abbey and Persuasion* (1818) · J. E. Austen-Leigh, *A memoir of Jane Austen* (1870); 2nd edn (1871) · W. Austen-Leigh and R. A. Austen-Leigh, *Jane Austen, her life and letters: a family record* (1913) · R. A. Austen-Leigh, ed., *Austen papers, 1704–1856* (1942) · C. Austen, *My aunt Jane Austen: a memoir* (1952) · W. Austen-Leigh and R. A. Austen-Leigh, *Jane Austen: a family record,* rev. D. Le Faye (1989); 2nd edn (2004) · D. Nokes, *Jane Austen: a life* (1997) · C. Tomalin, *Jane Austen: a life* (1997)

Literary and historical studies

R. Ballaster, *Women's worlds: ideology, femininity and the woman's magazine* (1991) · M. Butler, *Jane Austen and the war of ideas*

(1975) · C. Caplan and J. Breihan, 'Jane Austen and the militia', *Persuasions*, 14 (1992) · C. Caplan, 'Jane Austen's banker brother: Henry Thomas Austen of Austen & Co., 1801–1806', *Persuasions*, 20 (1998) · R. W. Chapman, *Jane Austen: facts and problems* (1948) · I. Collins, *Jane Austen and the clergy* (1994) · E. Copeland, *Women writing about money: women's fiction in England* (1995) · E. Copeland, 'Money', *The Cambridge companion to Jane Austen*, ed. E. Copeland and J. McMaster (1997) · L. Davidoff and C. Hall, *Family fortunes: men and women of the English middle-class, 1780–1850* (1987) · M. A. Doody, *The Rice portrait* (privately printed, 1996) · D. Le Faye, *Jane Austen's 'outlandish cousin': the life and letters of Eliza de Feuillide* (2002) · D. Le Faye, 'Chronology of Jane Austen's life', *The Cambridge companion to Jane Austen*, ed. E. Copeland and J. McMaster (1997) · D. Le Faye, 'A literary portrait re-examined: Jane Austen and Mary Anne Campion', *Book Collector*, 45 (1996), 508–25 · J. Fergus, 'Jane Austen: the professional woman writer', *The Cambridge companion to Jane Austen*, ed. E. Copeland and J. McMaster (1997) · P. Gay, *Jane Austen and the theatre* (2002) · D. Gilson, *A bibliography of Jane Austen* (1982); new edn (1997) · H. J. Habakkuk, *Marriage, debt and the estates system: English landownership, 1650–1950* (1994) · P. Honan, *Jane Austen: her life* (1987) · C. Johnson, 'Fair maid of Kent (the Rice portrait revisited)', *Times Literary Supplement* (13 March 1998) · D. Kaplan, 'Domesticity at sea: the example of Charles and Fanny Austen', *Persuasions*, 14 (1992) · B. Keith-Lucas, 'Francis and Francis Motley Austen, clerks of the peace for Kent', *Studies in modern Kentish history*, ed. A. Detsicas and N. Yates (1983), 87–102 · G. Keynes, *Jane Austen: a bibliography* (1929) · D. W. Smithers, *Jane Austen in Kent* (1981) · B. C. Southam, ed., *Jane Austen: the critical heritage*, 2 vols. (1968–87) · J. Todd, *The Cambridge introduction to Jane Austen* (2006) · G. H. Tucker, *A goodly heritage: a history of Jane Austen's family* (1983) · I. Watt, ed., *Jane Austen: a collection of critical essays* (1963)

Index